Book of Thoughts and Wisdom

by

Paul Hensche

DORRANCE
PUBLISHING CO
EST. 1920
PITTSBURGH, PENNSYLVANIA 15238

Dorrance Publishing Co
585 Alpha Drive
Suite 103
Pittsburgh, PA 15238
Visit our website at *www.dorrancebookstore.com*

ISBN: 978-1-4809-2005-7
eISBN 978-1-4809-2120-7

Introduction

Thoughts – Memories – Feelings

They are the measurement of all literature read, written, and listened to. These are the measurement of the subjects that have inspired me to write this literature.

I would like to give a special thanks to my wife, Beatrice, for her help, understanding, support and love for making this book possible.

Words of Thought

The true value of a friendship is in learning to respect each other's differences.
It doesn't mean you have to agree, only try to understand.
Remember…
Life is a test
It is only a test.

There's never nothing so sure today that tomorrow can't change it.
And all of the things we think are so important today, tomorrow they won't matter.
Remember…
Thank God for your blessings today.

Words of Thought

The difference between a mechanic and a technician:
A mechanic repairs,
A technician replaces.

Life is a journey;
It doesn't matter where
You've been or where you're going;
It's about who you share it with.

Words of Thought

Human Virtue

A human's strength and wisdom comes from God and lies within our human pride.

A human's greatness doesn't come from one's self; you must know who and what you are before you can find this happiness or contentment in life.

A human will only finds this happiness and contentment through the willingness of serving and helping others.

For this is God's will for human virtue.

Words of Thought
In Memory of Fellow Classmates

The Class of ___________

We are the Class of ____________.
Oh, how time has gone so fast, cherishing our memories of this past.
In children's games, we called our names,
with pushing, shoving, laughing, and crying.
We found our place in life's cruel game. All to be the Class of ____________.

The years went by, in time we grew; sharing and joining with others was new.
Friendships followed and teams were formed.
All to be the Class of __________.

We learned the rules of life, we did, with victories and losses at our feet.
With books of knowledge to fill our minds, goals of fortune and fame we seek.
Only to find this happiness at times so bleak.
In gathering together at times like this.
Rewarding this time with endless bliss. In remembering those who left us behind, cherishing their time through memory blinds.

When closing the book of life's great tests, in knowing the memories of our past.
Helped us through life's challenging tasks, for he or she who is the last
Will carry the greatest victory glass. For you will bring the trophy home
For the Class of _____________.
Dedicated to the Class of '65
Alden, Minnesota High School

Words of Thought

This Little Ring of Mine

This little ring of mine
Let it shine -- Let it shine

Haven't worn this ring for 50 years
This little ring of mine

It's old and tarnished just like me
This little ring of mine

It's a symbol of time and memories you see
This little ring of mine

It gives a bond to you and me
This little ring of mine

I polished it clean to be seen
This little ring of mine

It's on my hand it looks so grand
This little ring of mine

So Let it shine, Let it shine

Words of Thought
A Classmates Prayer

We've all written the letters in life,
of whom and what we've became.
but still needs a final say.

We think of times of the past,
to only wish they would last.

Knowing how our teachers and our class,
helped us through life's challenging tasks.

So when my time has come to pass,
I pray they too, remember my past.

I ask no thanks for what I write,
only to walk me to the sight.

When so asked to who this may be,
say a friend and a classmate you see.

Words of Thought
A Friendship Given

What is the value in a friendship? There is nothing greater in human life than a friendship given. It owes no debt, no scale, no measures its weight or price to measure its worth. It knows not jealousy, greed, or hate. Only love and compassion to whomever it is given.

So what is a friendship like this?

A God-given gift to us all to share.

For we danced the stars to sleep, we laughed till we cried, and now we cry till we hurt. You have left us all with these memories to cherish.

For everything there is a season.

A time for every matter under heaven,

A time to seek and a time to lose,

A time to plant and a time to harvest,

A time to weep and a time to laugh,

A time to mourn and a time to dance,

A time to be born and a time to die,

So, too, there is a time for coming together and a time for parting,

Thank you, my friend, for sharing this time.

For memories live on forever.

Friendship never dies.

In memory of Ramond Lapp

Words of Thought
Special Friends

There's never such a thing as just a dog or cat
if they're your best friend and you love them.
They have no precious silver or gold, for only we have this to hold.
They ask for only love and time, a precious gift in this world to find.
An unconditional love they share, in looking for your loving care.
Thank God for special friends like these.
For only he knows their special love.

Words of Thought
A Mother's Love

There's no greater blessing on earth than the gift of a mother's love.
As a farmer plants his seed of life, so too you carry this seed of life.
To nourish, to guide throughout your life.
A womb so warm, it knows not cold
An innocence so pure, the world not known
A protection is given, to secure this life
A sacrifice is given, to save this life
A touch of life, before all others
A forgiving pain so loud and bold
A dream to wonder and yet not be known
To what the future may behold
These are a few of the things we're told
That only a mother's love can behold
So let's thank God for this blessed gift
For only a mother can give this gift.

A Mother's Love
Happy Mother's Day

Dedicated to my mother, Norma Hensche

Words of Thought
Whitney Houston

A voice so blessed, you listen in awe,
To find that spirit within us all.
A smile so bright, a radiance of light,
With eyes of sparkle to our sight.
A heart and soul so warm, indeed,
With a gift of comfort in a world of need.
A star so bright the world could see,
Praying this light could always be.
A falling star, the world would say,
And yet so bright in its passing way.
For in your darkest hour of light,
Not even demons could stop your flight.
For Jesus heard you call his name
And took you from your endless pain.
God bless you, Whitney, for sharing your life,
A gift he gave to remind us all
That in the end he loves us all.

I look to you.

In memory of Whitney Houston

Words of Thought
Marriage

(God's special gift)

For this reason man and woman,
leave their mother and father,
and are joined as one.

To love and to cherish, so is told.

The days grow long, the nights grow cold,
To love and to cherish, so is told.

The patience grows short and the anger grows bold,
To love and to cherish, so is told.

The money grows short, the worry grows long,
To love and to cherish, so is told.

In sickness and health, so the bible tells,
To love and to cherish, so is told.

So through these times of trouble and trials,
I'll love and cherish.

(God's special gift)

Words of Thought
A Christmas Gift

It's this time of the year,
we like to share with family,
and friends that are so dear;
to share the gift of love,
by having them so near.

Life not always makes this so clear,
but still hold this thought so dear.

For there memories live on forever,
and their friendship never dies,

God's gift is always near.

Words of Thought
A Young Farm Boy's Dream

What makes a farm boy's dreams real? Maybe it's that first tractor ride, the first ride in the old farm pickup truck, or that first walk to the barn with Dad with that new toy tractor in hand. Whatever it is, it lays the foundation for a farm boy's dream that will never end.

That scary ride on that big tractor for the first time, looking at those big tires going around and around so fast, along with sitting so high in the air, makes you hang on to the strong arm that is holding you so tight. Then when the tractor stops and you get off, your first words are, can we do this again?

Then there's that first ride in the old noisy pickup truck, not knowing where you're going, just hoping Dad knows how to get back. As you're looking out the back window at the farm, you sit on the edge of the seat, just being able to see over the dash. All of a sudden, a town appears, so you ask, where are we going? A stern voice answers back, to the implement shop. Well, not knowing what an implement shop is, you sit with excitement, because if it is anything like that tractor ride, you know it is going to be fun.

Then you reach town and, turning the corner, you see all of those tractors all lined up, ready to take for a drive. So you ask, can we drive them? Then that terrible word you hear: no. We've got to go inside and get some parts. I think to myself, whatever that is. So once inside, there are even more tractors. Then the magic words I hear: You can sit on the tractors, but be careful. So I am. After making all of those powerful engine noises, I see Dad come with a bag in his hand, and he says those other terrible words: Let's go! So we do and sure enough, we find our way back home.

Then evening comes, and it is time to eat supper. After supper I am asked if I want to go to the barn to play while milking is being done. Well, after a hard day of driving those tractors, I am getting tired. But with wide-open eyes, I am ready to go. Then at the door, Dad stops me and says, If you're going to play, you might need this. He reaches in that parts bag and pulls out a new toy tractor. My eyes get even bigger. So with tractor tight in hand, out the door to the barn we go, with a grin on my face from ear to ear, trying to follow in those footsteps. (I now know what "going after parts" means.) A corner in the alley of the barn, next to the straw, makes a good shed for my tractor to store. Playing in the manger next to the cows. Climbing the hills and farming the feed (pretending it's dirt). Then making the noise of that powerful tractor makes this seem all so real.

In a farm boy's dream, the night goes on, the farming is done, so to the shed I go with tractor in hand, only to find it occupied. (That mean old cat, I think.) So quickly I make another. After lying down to rest a while, I hear a voice to my surprise. Bring your tractor; we've finished it all. With tractor in hand, eyes hardly open, stumbling in those footsteps back again, I go to bed, say my prayers, and fall asleep, knowing there's only two things in a farm boy's dream. Tractors and chores. And to do them tomorrow again, hoping this dream will never end.

An Old Farm Boy

Words of Thought
The Working Man

God bless the working man with calloused hands and twisted fingers.
He leaves his work upon this land, with scars and sores so untold.

He builds our homes to shelter our lives
with skilled hands to show his pride.

He builds the roads and bridges we see
only to carry our every need.

He makes the tools to build and repair,
an endless job in the world of care.

He drives equipment so big and small,
all with danger behind each wall.

He teaches our children in learning of all
to replace and care for us all.

He protects and serves with his life to all,
only to find he is so small.

He tries to show his caring side in sharing his life with his bride,
while trying to keep his manly pride.

So when his time has come to rest
he knows he's done his very best.

For in his hands the story tells,
God has blessed
The Working Man.

Words of Thought
Time

What is time to us all?

It has not a price to be bought or sold,
For only in seasons to unfold.
It knows not sorrow, hate, or love,
For only through your eyes this is to behold.
It spares not one from strife or pain,
For only through this we find our gain.
It knows not mourning to the young so dear,
For only time will make this clear.
It's not ours to give or to take,
For only ours to celebrate.

So what is time to us all?

A God-given gift in a time glass so clear,
Through good times and bad times,
Our thoughts of time bring us so near.
For we are family.
This is so clear.

In memory of Charles Hensche family.

Words of Thought
We've Done It All

A Poem of Truth

There's no power like Red Power.
If it's not Red, leave it in the shed.

That's our motto: I am an International Harvester Man. Some say we're prejudice and some say we are no more, and that's okay, but let me say we've done it all.

We farmed the world with pride and joy and still had time to make the toys.

We milked the cows and separated the cream, kept it cool and trucked it away. We've done it all with the Harvester name.

We made the hay, filled the silos, and spread the crap; we've done it all with the Harvester name.

We cleaned the house, cooked the meals, and kept the ice cream cool from melting away in the heat of the day. We've done it all with the Harvester name.

We mowed the grass, made the roads, trucked the dirt, loaded the sand, and moved the snow. Hell! We've done it all with the Harvester name.

We plowed the fields and harvested the crops. Yes, we've done it all with the Harvester name.
So Mr. Greenjeans, when you, Billy-Bob, and Charlene were chugging along, the whole town said it was wrong. They were screaming it should have been Red. They knew the world was being changed, by bussing your children with the Harvester name. So you may say we are no more, and the future's yours to roar. But let me say, without a doubt, the Harvester name is forevermore, for Mr. Greenjeans, we've done it all.

The International Harvester Man

Words of Thought
(Brothers in Red)

The IH Red Power Machine

We gather together with tribute in hand, remembering a company and its men. They designed and built the very best.
The IH Red Power Machine

With sweating brow and hands of steel, they opened the earth to find its ore. They forged it hot and machined it smooth. They bolted it tight and welded it strong, all showing their pride in what they did.
The IH Red Power Machine

A moment of truth tells it all with a pull of the throttle and a breath of fire. It rose from the floor with a great roar! Standing in awe, the world could see the best there was.
The IH Red Power Machine

Leaving the door with shining pride. Standing in line to serve mankind. Big or small, they earned the name.
The IH Red Power Machine

Five million strong we stand one day. Being the first the world has seen. Thanks to the men of this time. They built the best in such little time.
The IH Red Power Machine
Though the mills are quite and the stacks run cold, you opened doors to behold and gave us memories we can hold. For there is no line for
The IH Red Power Machine

As Brothers in Red we gather together, sharing this common bond
There's No Power Like Red Power
For we are the Roar to
The IH Red Power Machine

Let not history dust its feet off on a company and men, who did so much for mankind at a time in history when so much was needed and so little to be gotten.

International Harvester Was There for All

Words of Thought
Big Red

Big Red is my name and power is my game.
We have no shame in the International Harvester Name.
Big or small, new or old
We powered the world with pride and fame.
They painted us gray for many a year, waiting for someone to shed this tear.
A stroke of a pen and a wave of a brush made us red, then called us by name, "Big Red."
We took no crap from other names. "Tougher the better" was our game.
They coffee talk this and they coffee that, but track or field everybody feared "Big Red."
There was no ground we couldn't turn or no task too tough to pass.
Field to yard we did it all, "Big Red."
We led the world to where it is, only to find unforgiving times.
With a stroke of a pen and a wave of a brush, history speaks in changing times
And sheds a tear of the past to find the future in our grasp.
No matter how history deals its hand, there is no future without a past.
Memories now we can behold in future calling as so bold, "Big Red."
With pride and honor we're given this name
For only we have shared its pain.

Big Red

1936: Farmall tractors are painted red for safety reasons, replacing their familiar gray color. This marks the beginning of "Big Red."

Words of Thought

Life is a journey;
It doesn't matter where
You've been or where you're going.
It's about who you share it with.

Words of Thought
Life at Death

When in time you feel life
is nearing its end,

know this–it's just beginning.

With God there is no time, no hour,
no day, no week, no month, no year,
no pain, no sorrow.

Eternity is forever.
For what we live is just a test,
only a test!

Words of Thought
Life

Life is not about where we have been or where we are going, for our greatest joy comes from with whom we share this trip, for as the sparrows and the trees know their seasons. Everything under heaven has its time and its place.

A time to plant and a time to harvest
A time to cry and a time to laugh
A time to mourn and a time to dance
A time to seek and a time to hold.
A time to worry and a time to smile

So, too, there was a time for us to come together and now a time to say goodbye, for in this time we shared many things, not knowing what tomorrow will bring, for only through death do we see these things and find the value that life brings.

Goodbye for now.